Welcome to
LifeSearch!

If you urgently need to prepare to lead a LifeSearch group, turn the page and read QuickLead. QuickLead will give you enough information to get started.

LifeSearch hopes to help you and other persons within a small group explore topics about which you are concerned in your everyday living. We've tried to make LifeSearch

✔ immediately helpful to you;

✔ filled with practical ideas;

✔ Christian-oriented and biblically based;

✔ group building, so you will find companions in your mutual struggles and learning;

✔ easy for anyone to lead.

You have probably chosen to join with others in studying this LifeSearch book because you feel some need. You may feel that need in your life strongly. Our hope for you is that by the time you complete the six chapters in this book with your LifeSearch group, you will have

✔ a better handle on how to meet the need you feel;

✔ some greater insights into yourself;

✔ a deeper understanding of how Christian faith can help you meet that need;

✔ a more profound relationship with God;

✔ new and/or richer relationships with the other persons in your LifeSearch group.

If you discover nothing else as part of this LifeSearch experience, we want you to learn this fact: *that you are not alone as you face life*. Other people have faced and still face the same problems, struggles, demands, and needs that you face. Some have advice to offer. Some have learned things the hard way— things they can now tell you about. Some can help you think through and talk through old concerns and new insights. Some can listen as you share what you've tried and what you want to achieve. Some even need what you can offer.

And you will never be alone because God stands with you.

The secret to LifeSearch is in the workings of your group. No two LifeSearch groups will ever be alike. Your LifeSearch group is made up of unique individuals— including you. All of you have much to offer one another. This Life-Search book simply provides a framework for you and your group to work together in learning about an area of mutual concern.

We would like to hear what you think about LifeSearch and ways you can suggest for improving future LifeSearch books. A Mail-In Feedback survey appears in the back. Whether you lead the group or participate in it, please take the time to fill out the survey and mail it in to us.

IF YOU ARE LEADING A Life-Search GROUP, please read the articles in the back of this book. These LifeSearch group leadership articles may answer the questions you have about leading your group.

IF YOU ARE PARTICIPATING IN A LifeSearch GROUP, BUT NOT LEADING IT, please read at least the article, "If You're Not Leading the Group." In any case, **you will benefit most if you come to your group meeting having read the chapter ahead of time and having attempted any assignments given in the previous chapter's "Before Next Time" sections.**

We want to remain helpful to you throughout your LifeSearch group experience. If you have any questions about using this LifeSearch book, please feel free to call Curric-U-Phone at 1-800-251-8591, and ask for the LifeSearch editor.

QUICKLEAD™

Look here for **QUICK** information about how to **LEAD** a session of LIFE-SEARCH. On LIFESEARCH pages, look for the following:

ICONS
Seven kinds of icons suggest different kinds of activities for your group to do at different points during the session (see page 4 for more information about ICONS).

MAIN TEXT: the "meat" of the session. Hopefully everyone will have read the MAIN TEXT ahead of time; if not, be prepared to offer a brief summary of the MAIN TEXT in your own words.

MARGINAL NOTES give you activity instructions and additional discussion starters.

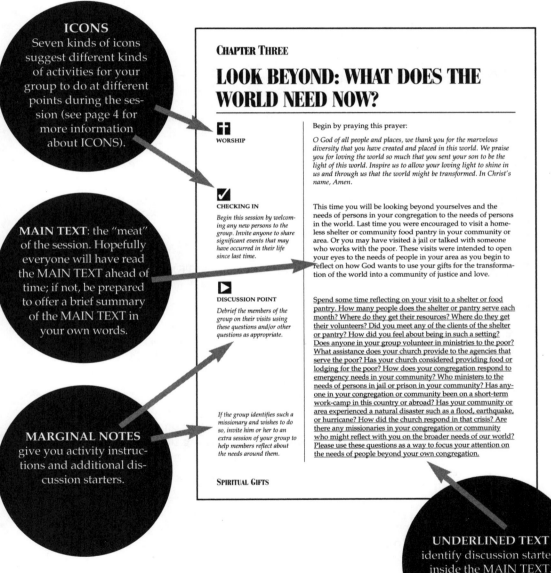

CHAPTER THREE

LOOK BEYOND: WHAT DOES THE WORLD NEED NOW?

WORSHIP

Begin by praying this prayer:

O God of all people and places, we thank you for the marvelous diversity that you have created and placed in this world. We praise you for loving the world so much that you sent your son to be the light of this world. Inspire us to allow your loving light to shine in us and through us that the world might be transformed. In Christ's name, Amen.

CHECKING IN

Begin this session by welcoming any new persons to the group. Invite anyone to share significant events that may have occurred in their life since last time.

This time you will be looking beyond yourselves and the needs of persons in your congregation to the needs of persons in the world. Last time you were encouraged to visit a homeless shelter or community food pantry in your community or area. Or you may have visited a jail or talked with someone who works with the poor. These visits were intended to open your eyes to the needs of people in your area as you begin to reflect on how God wants to use your gifts for the transformation of the world into a community of justice and love.

DISCUSSION POINT

Debrief the members of the group on their visits using these questions and/or other questions as appropriate.

Spend some time reflecting on your visit to a shelter or food pantry. How many people does the shelter or pantry serve each month? Where do they get their resources? Where do they get their volunteers? Did you meet any of the clients of the shelter or pantry? How did you feel about being in such a setting? Does anyone in your group volunteer in ministries to the poor? What assistance does your church provide to the agencies that serve the poor? Has your church considered providing food or lodging for the poor? How does your congregation respond to emergency needs in your community? Who ministers to the needs of persons in jail or prison in your community? Has anyone in your congregation or community been on a short-term work-camp in this country or abroad? Has your community or area experienced a natural disaster such as a flood, earthquake, or hurricane? How did the church respond in that crisis? Are there any missionaries in your congregation or community who might reflect with you on the broader needs of our world? Please use these questions as a way to focus your attention on the needs of people beyond your own congregation.

If the group identifies such a missionary and wishes to do so, invite him or her to an extra session of your group to help members reflect about the needs around them.

SPIRITUAL GIFTS

UNDERLINED TEXT identify discussion starters inside the MAIN TEXT.

For more information, read the **LEADERSHIP ARTICLES** in the back of this LIFESEARCH book.

ICONS

ICONS are picture/symbols that show you at a glance what you should do with different parts of the main text at different times in the LifeSearch sessions.

The seven kinds of icons are

 WORSHIP—A prayer, hymn, or other act of worship is suggested at this place in the MAIN TEXT.

 CHECKING IN—At the beginning of each session, LifeSearch group members will be asked to "check in" with each other about what is happening in their lives. Sometimes group members will also be asked to "check in" about how their LifeSearch group experience seems to them.

 DISCUSSION POINT—Either the MAIN TEXT or a MARGINAL NOTE will suggest discussion starters. You will probably find more DIS-CUSSION POINTS than you can use in the usual LifeSearch session.

 GROUP INTERACTION—Either the MAIN TEXT or a MARGINAL NOTE will suggest a group activity that goes beyond a simple discussion within the whole group.

 BIBLE STUDY—At least once each session, your LifeSearch group will study a Bible passage together. Usually, DISCUSSION POINTS and/or GROUP INTERACTIONS are part of the BIBLE STUDY.

 WRITTEN REFLECTION—The MAIN TEXT will contain one or more suggestions for individuals to reflect personally on an issue. Space will be provided within the MAIN TEXT for writing down reflections. Sometimes individuals will be invited to share their written reflections if they wish.

 BEFORE NEXT TIME—In most sessions, your LifeSearch group members will be asked to do something on their own before the next time you meet together.

INTRODUCTION

Wholeness

If we could ask Jesus, "What must I do to be a whole person?" how would he reply? The Gospels do not record anyone asking Jesus what it is to be whole—but suppose we restate the question. What must I do to be a whole person? How do I find fulfillment? What am I put on this earth to do? What is the prime rule that I must follow?

"One of the scribes came near and heard them disputing with one another, and seeing that he answered them well, he asked him, 'Which commandment is the first of all?' Jesus answered, 'The first is, "Hear, O Israel: the Lord our God, the Lord is one; you shall love the Lord your God with all your heart, and with all your soul, and with all your mind, and with all your strength." The second is this, "You shall love your neighbor as yourself." There is no other commandment greater than these' " (Mark 12:28-31).

In the time of Jesus, a *scribe* was a learned man who understood and respected the law and who was trained to interpret it. Many times in the New Testament, scribes are portrayed as opposing Jesus. But this unnamed scribe was different. He was not trying to trap Jesus. He was asking the teacher a question—the most important question there can be. And his heart was prepared to receive the answer.

Jesus answered the scribe by quoting two ancient commandments. The first, the *Shema* ("Hear, O Israel . . .") expresses the core of Judaism. The second commandment (". . .love your neighbor as yourself,") like the *Shema*, comes from the Book of Deuteronomy. In his answer, Jesus linked the love of God, love of neighbor, and love of oneself. The answer to the scribe's question, the answer to *our* question, is love—the magnificent, overpowering love that flows from recognition of God, the love that is the quest for reconciliation with God.

That reconciliation is known as "atonement." In modern English, atonement connotes mostly the idea of making reparation—what we in the nineties might think of as "payback." But the biblical meaning of atonement is "reunification with God." That can be better recognized in the Middle English origins of the word: atonement, or "at-one-ment," specifically, being "at one" with God. Perhaps the modern English word that best captures this meaning is *wholeness*.

Would not Jesus answer our question— "What must I do to be a whole person?"—as he did the scribe's? So let Jesus' reply determine our meaning for *wholeness*. Wholeness is found in obeying the greatest commandment.

You might want to reread the whole story of the scribe as told in Mark 12:28-34. After hearing Jesus' answer to his question, the scribe recognized its truth and affirmed that indeed that was the correct way to live. Jesus saw that the man understood and told him, "You are not far from the kingdom of God" (Mark 12:34).

Health

The Scriptures do not speak as directly to the meaning of *health*. But in a famous parable (Luke 19:11-27), Jesus talks about something that has come to be known as *stewardship*. The good steward (manager) entrusted with a business or property certainly does not diminish it, nor does he merely preserve it. Instead he develops it so that it is even more valuable after his care. The Book of 1 Peter speaks of the impor-tance of good stewardship of the gifts God has given us (1 Peter 4:10). One of those gifts is your physical being—your body.

The dictionary defines *health* as the "state of optimal functioning of an organism." For a Christian, then, "health" can be thought of as steward-ship over the gift of our bodies.

And to what end do we put our bodies? To what end do we pursue health? To what other end than wholeness! That is to live the answer that Jesus gave to the scribe—to love!

—Dr. Bart Resta

Dr. Bart Resta is a husband, father, and pediatrician living in Clarksville, Tennessee. A graduate of Johns Hopkins University and Ohio State University, he completed his residency at Childrens Hospital in Los Angeles. Currently he is assistant professor of pediatrics at Meharry Medical College in Nashville, Tennessee, and maintains a practice at Metropolitan Nashville General Hospital. Though as yet unpublished, Dr. Resta enjoys writing children's stories. He and his family are members of Madison Street United Methodist Church in Clarksville.

CHAPTER ONE

THE JOY OF LIFE

CHECKING IN

The gathering time helps build community and encourages a climate for open and honest sharing. At this time each session you will get to know other members by sharing about events from the past week. Take time now to have persons introduce themselves with names and one expectation they have for being a part of this LIFE-SEARCH group exploring health and wholeness. You may want to take notes on newsprint so that at your last session you can see how many expectations were met.

Let us celebrate the joy of health and wholeness! The scent of a rose, the song of a bird, the warmth of the sun on my face—these simple pleasures I know because God has given me a body that can sense them. When I read a book or hug my child, when I accomplish a goal, even when I fail at a task, I do all these things with and through my human body.

To be human is to change. A single cell becomes a baby; the baby becomes a child; the child becomes an adult; the adult grows old. Injury, disease, and degeneration inevitably belie the promise of youth. Our bodies are imperfect and must eventually fail us completely.

But the other side of that coin is that, just as our bodies change from childhood to old age, so too do we mature in our gifts, our skills, and our capacity to know God. Today let us focus on the wonderful things that our bodies allow us to do.

WORSHIP

Use the part of Psalm 100 printed in the main text as a prayer for your group to read together.

Make a joyful noise to the LORD,
all the earth.
Worship the LORD with gladness;
come into his presence with singing.

Know that the LORD is God.
It is he that made us, and we are his;
we are his people, and the
sheep of his pasture.

For the LORD is good;
his steadfast love endures forever,
and his faithfulness to all generations.
(Psalm 100: 1-3,5)

WRITTEN REFLECTION

As you begin this LIFESEARCH study, privately consider the following questions. Write your reflections in the spaces provided.

What concerns do you have relating to health and wholeness? What questions would you like the group to address as you move together through the sessions?

If you need additional space to write your "present blessings," use the margins or write your blessings on a separate piece of paper.

How has God blessed you? What gives you pleasure? What do you enjoy doing? From base sensation to lofty undertakings, what do you have to thank God for? This is your list of "present blessings." Make it as long as you like!

DISCUSSION POINT

Ask group members to share answers to the first question. Then compare lists of blessings. Which blessings are shared?

Which are more unique?

In what ways has your body been, and might continue to be, a blessing for you?

Be prepared to share some of your responses with your LIFE-SEARCH group.

The Voyage of Life

In one way, we can say that our lives began when the seeds of life from our biologic fathers and mothers united. In that instant, ancient genes reformed into a new being, truly alive, truly human, truly unique, but almost unrecognizably different from what we are now. That fertilized egg was a tiny, fragile ship carrying the thought, the plan, for a new human being into the world.

Planted in the proper soil, given the proper care, a seed in a garden has a chance to develop into something magnificent. So it is with the human seed, also. That tiny cell can grow into an Einstein, a Mozart, or a Mother Theresa; it can blossom into a loving mother or a beloved son. But not all soils support such growth, and too often human lives are lost or wasted when the needs of the developing person are not met.

The changes that take place between conception and birth are miraculous. The fertilized egg divides and then grows, divides and grows, into a ball of cells—the embryo. A complex chemical dance takes place between hormones from the embryo and the mother, and a place is prepared in the womb for the tiny being. The placenta develops from the embryo, and it serves as the link between the developing baby and its mother. By the end of the third week, the primitive heart has begun to beat, and the various other organ systems are forming and beginning to function as well.

All the body systems are differentiated by the beginning of the third month. The remaining months of intrauterine life are characterized by rapid growth of the baby as he is nourished by his mother. His weight increases from approximately two ounces at three months to (usually) five to ten pounds at birth. As the fetus completes that growth, additional changes take place in both mother and baby to prepare them for the challenge of birth.

Birth marks the end of the infant's total dependence on her mother's body. Although far from completely mature, the newborn infant can now live and move and grow away from the mother. But now begins another process as important—or perhaps more important— to the wholeness of that baby as continued proper physical development. For the infant has been born into a family and community of other human beings. With birth begins the process of socialization.

And how does the baby begin? With a smile! By about six weeks of age the infant learns to return a smile. Soon she learns to make others smile by smiling herself. She and her mother study and influence each other. The infant comes to see her mother as a specific person (as *her* specific person), and vice versa. This new human being discovers love.

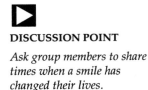

DISCUSSION POINT

Ask group members to share times when a smile has changed their lives.

What a marvelous blessing is this gift of a smile! Was it on anyone's list of blessings that come from having a human body? For no other species can smile like we do!

As the baby becomes a child, he continues to grow and mature physically. In time, he can roll over, and crawl, and walk. His senses become acute. He begins to reach for and grasp objects. Soon he can feed himself.

Now social development predominates over physical development. The toddler learns how to accommodate his parent's needs, just as the mother and father adapt to his. His efforts at communication, which began with glances and cries, soon progress to words.

More than anything in the world, this little bundle of energy wants to be like her parents. She imitates everything she sees. Even when she fights her parents, she is struggling to be independent—like they are. She takes into herself her parents' meanings for good and bad. She begins to contemplate what she does. She develops a conscience.

Relatively little physical change takes place in the school-age child, except for growth in height and weight. But this stage is characterized by many social, intellectual, and emotional challenges. He develops more of a sense of self, and separates more from his parents. He learns to live with many different individuals, and he learns to become a member of groups other than his family. He gains the self-esteem and confidence that comes with acquisition of a variety of skills, including reading, writing, and all kinds of play.

Bodily change occurs again in the teen years, as the hormonal signals of puberty trigger not only the internal maturation of the reproductive system, but also the secondary sexual characteristics, such as body hair, the size and appearance of the genitalia, breast development, and changes in the voice. The same hormones also bring about an end to growth in height.

These changes play havoc with the adolescent's sense of identity. All she has known is being a girl; now she has a new and awkward body and confused thoughts. People view her differently; many look at her and see a woman, her parents still see their little girl. She is a girl; she is a woman; she is both. She must learn to accept her new self, she must cope with having a sexual nature, she must separate from her parents, by rebellion if necessary, in order to become an independent adult. A tall order indeed!

▶

DISCUSSION POINT

It can be hard for parents to remember that children are *supposed* to separate from them. How did your parents handle this issue with you? What advice would you have for teens or their parents based on your experience?

Most of us make it through adolescence, although many do not have good memories of that time. In contrast, many older people do fondly recall their early adulthood. By then the challenges of the teen years have been met.

For most, this is the time of learning a trade or going to college. This is the time of taking on the identity of a profession—of becoming a teacher, a carpenter, a homemaker, a musician. We are defined on the basis of what we do. And at this stage, for a time, we are happy with that.

Now the focus is not on separation from family, but on creation of new family, new friends, new ties. Young men and women may search for a partner with whom to share their lives. They want to experience love again. For many, marriage fulfills that longing. Others may search for love and meaning in work, a vocation, or other relationships. Soon, some of this generation become parents, and the cycle starts anew.

But the life of the first generation does not end when the second is born. Now one must meet the material and spiritual challenges of raising a family. There is never enough time, never enough money, never enough patience. And the workplace often seems more forceful in demanding one's attention than does one's family.

Slowly for some, more rapidly for others, another force begins to appear in our lives. Our bodies, which have seemed unchanging for decades, begin to deteriorate. At first we pay little heed to our weakening vision or the ringing in our ears. But our bodies do weaken. Muscles become a little less strong, bones a little more fragile. It's harder to remember things. The skin begins to wrinkle; the joints begin to ache. As the changes accumulate, the chance of a real disaster grows. For example, a slight elevation in blood pressure, coupled with mild diabetes, plus, say, a weakness for the wrong kind of desserts, can greatly increase the odds of a heart attack.

DISCUSSION POINT

It is said of children and adolescents that they are reckless because they think they will live forever. How did you become aware of your own mortality? How has your sense of mortality affected the way you care for yourself?

When we have reached the peak of our powers, just as we are about to enjoy the fruits of career and family, our bodies let us down. We begin to realize that it will be an unrelenting process. We confront the idea of mortality. We all—our friends, our spouses, ourselves—must inevitably weaken and die.

WRITTEN REFLECTION

These words are what I might say to my growing child. Using a separate piece of paper or margins, write what you would say to yours.

Child, you grew up so much faster than I did! Just yesterday I was rocking you beside the Christmas tree. Now you're grown up and gone. And I am old now, no doubt about it anymore. Sooner or later—a lot sooner than I once thought—I am going to die. But the strange thing is, I don't seem to mind the idea of dying, now.

DISCUSSION POINT

How well does this hymn capture your prayer for children?

Child of Blessing, Child of Promise

*Child of blessing, child of promise,
baptized with the Spirit's sign;
with this water God has sealed you
unto love and grace divine.*

*Child of love, our love's expression,
love's creation, loved indeed!
Fresh from God, refresh our spirits,
into joy and laughter lead.*

*Child of joy, our dearest treasure,
God's you are, from God you came.
Back to God we humbly give you;
live as one who bears Christ's name.*

*Child of God your loving Parent,
learn to know whose child you are.
Grow to laugh and sing and worship,
trust and love God more than all.*

WRITTEN REFLECTION

Use the margin or a separate piece of paper to record blessings.

Refer back to your list of present blessings. Now make two additional lists, labeled "past blessings" and "future blessings." <u>What did you enjoy in your youth? What do you look forward to in old age? With which blessings from your past would you like to reacquaint yourself?</u>

DISCUSSION POINT

Compare your lists with those of others in the group.

<u>How do your lists seem to change with the passage of time? How does your stage of life affect your blessings?</u>

Encountering Scripture

BIBLE STUDY

Ask members of the group to share or summarize what they can remember from the whole of the Sermon on the Mount (Matthew 5–7).

This selection is from the Sermon on the Mount. The introduction to the sermon given in Matthew 4:23-25 tells us that large crowds of people, from lands that today make up at least three countries (Israel, Syria, and Jordan), came to hear Jesus speak. Included among them were many who were ill with various diseases. Many must have been poor. Jesus rewarded their persistence in coming to him with some of the most beautiful words ever spoken.

GROUP INTERACTION

Assign the roles listed in the main text to members of the group to roleplay. Ask them to think about what their character might think and feel as you read aloud Matthew 6:25-33.

Ask members to use their role to present their reaction to the group. Then, continuing in their roles, ask them to discuss the Rabbi's sermon.

Next, shedding the roles, ask everyone to discuss the meaning of Jesus' words for their lives today.

BEFORE NEXT TIME

WORSHIP

You may wish to sing these words, No. 405 in The United Methodist Hymnal (The United Methodist Publishing House, 1989).

Pretend that you are part of that great crowd gathered to hear Jesus. Perhaps you have travelled for many weeks, pushed through that mass of humanity, and now you sit close enough to the Rabbi to touch his cloak. Pretend that you are one of the following:

John, the disciple whom Jesus loved.

A healthy, muscular Roman centurion, curious about this Galilean.

A blind woman, who was now healed by Jesus, and who since has been following him.

A young boy paralyzed in a fall, whose father, hoping for a miracle, has brought him to Jesus.

An adolescent girl, crippled and in great pain from arthritis in all her joints. She has followed Jesus, but she has not been cured.

An old, old man, obviously close to death.

What do Jesus' words mean to you? Can you believe them?

Before you meet with your group next time, read Job 3:20-23. Ask yourself whether those words reflect your feelings presently or sometime during the past.

As you prepare to end this session, share with one another prayer concerns or joys. Record those in the space below:

Read these words from Matthew 6:33 (King James Version):

"Seek ye first the kingdom of God, and his righteousness; and all these things shall be added unto you." Allelu!

CHAPTER TWO

HUMAN SUFFERING

WORSHIP

Read these words aloud as you begin your session.

Why is light given to one in misery,
and life to the bitter in soul,
who long for death, but it does not come,
and dig for it more than for hidden
treasures;
who rejoice exceedingly,
and are glad when they find the grave?
Why is light given to one who
cannot see the way,
whom God has fenced in?
(Job 3:20-23.)

Some suffering we share; some we keep hidden. If you or a loved one are suffering, you may wish to share your pain with your LIFESEARCH group before or as you pray. Use the space below to record the concerns of your group.

As you invite group members to share, remind the group of a basic covenant: Information of a personal nature is shared for the purpose of prayer. It is not to be discussed with persons who are not a part of the LIFESEARCH group.

In unison, pray:

My God, my God, why have you forsaken me?
Why are you so far from helping me,
from the words of my groaning?
O my God, I cry by day, but you
do not answer;
and by night, but find no rest.
(Psalm 22:1-2.)

DISCUSSION POINT

How can I live with such pain? Is there any sense to it? Why did God do this to me?

Today we talk about human suffering—about disease, injury, degeneration, and death. Every human being experiences moments of physical suffering. Babies cry long before they smile. We all cope with illness and injury. Some of us must spend all of our energy in combat against a disease or disability. All of us eventually face death.

There are other kinds of suffering that we know well—emotional and spiritual suffering. We can feel the pain of others. When our loved ones suffer, we suffer with them. The death of a parent, child, or friend can steal joy from our lives. When what we have loved is no more, we hurt terribly. Because God created us with great abilities to think, many of us seek answers to spiritual and emotional turmoil.

Consider a Disease

WRITTEN REFLECTION

Consider a disease, illness, or disability that you know well—either through experiencing it personally or by living with a loved one who has. Reflect on these questions, writing your thoughts in the spaces below:

How does it affect the body? If there is pain, what is it like? What physical limitations are imposed? How does it change the patient's body-image?

How does the illness affect one's perception of life? What former joys are limited or cut off by it? How does it change the way the patient relates to others?

How are other people affected by the illness? How does it change the way they relate to the patient? Are some relationships particularly vulnerable?

DISCUSSION POINT

Divide the larger group into groups of twos or threes. Ask the smaller groups to share their written reflections. What similarities are there in your responses?

How does the illness affect one's relationship with God?

When students in the health professions study pathology, they learn that an organism responds to diverse diseases through a relatively limited number of pathways. A burn, an insect bite, an infection—all can trigger the redness, swelling, and pain of the inflammatory response. Do different kinds of illnesses cause similar emotional or spiritual damage?

Different Kinds of Pain

You cannot escape pain in the hospital. Even though one can have surgery without feeling the knife, even though analgesics can deaden the pangs of childbirth, even though the terminal patient can gently slide into death in a narcotic fog—the pain is still there. For those who have been in the hospital a long time, the pain is almost constant.

It is there at night, when it steals your sleep. The doctors and nurses may wake you up, but pain wakes you the most. Sleep often comes only twenty or thirty minutes at a time, and that kind of sleep cannot restore you.

It is there in the morning, when that cheerful technician wakes you up (though you were not really asleep) to draw your blood. Your veins are not what they used to be. Three attempts and then they send for someone else to try.

The pain is there later when the doctors come by, when you cannot understand what they are saying, when all you can understand is "more tests."

16

The pain returns when visiting hours come. There are no visitors, and it hurts. If visitors come, that hurts too. No one knows what to say. You don't know what to say. You have become skilled at small talk. It hurts. The pain is there when you anticipate paying the bill for all the pain. A lengthy hospitalization can erode the savings of a lifetime, particularly when insurance coverage is slim.

For terminally ill patients, the pain is there when you think about your family not being able to manage without you—or worse, being able to manage without you.

The pain is there in the evening, when you realize that another day has gone by, but you are no closer to going home.

The pain is there when you ask why this has happened to you.

Case Studies

1. A baby, otherwise perfect, is born fifteen weeks too early. She weighs only one pound. Her parents want the medical personnel to do everything possible to save her. In spite of "heroic measures," she dies three days later.

2. Another baby with the same degree of prematurity survives, and is able to leave the hospital after a six-month stay. He suffers several of the known complications of prematurity—he is blind, at least moderately retarded, and has cerebral palsy.

3. A promising young medical student suffers a spinal cord injury in a sledding accident. At the age of twenty, she is paralyzed from the neck down.

4. The mother of four children is admitted for routine tests to evaluate her chest pain. In the midst of testing she suffers cardiac arrest. She cannot be resuscitated.

5. A former pastor develops Alzheimer's disease. Gradually it progresses, until, for the last two years of his life, he does not recognize his family, let alone recall that he spent fifty years in service to God and humanity. His wife is too weak to care for him, so he must be institutionalized.

6. A woman lives to be one hundred years old. She suffers no overwhelming physical pain, and she dies peacefully in her sleep one night. But her husband was the only person she ever loved, and he died twenty-five years before. She has spent the last quarter-century in mourning for him.

GROUP INTERACTION

Divide your LIFESEARCH group into small groups of three to five persons. Each smaller group should choose one of these case studies—all based on actual cases—to study. Each group should consider the questions in the main text following the set of case studies.

DISCUSSION POINT

It is painful to consider such situations when we come upon them in real life. It is a natural response to turn away. But if we do, we may expect that others will turn away when we suffer, too.

1. What is consumed in this suffering? What, if anything, will remain afterwards for those involved?

2. What would be the normal, human response to having such a situation thrust upon you? How do you hope you would respond? How do you guess you would react? Is there a gap between how you wish you would respond and how you think you would respond?

3. Could any person blame you for being overwhelmed by this situation?

4. Could *God* blame you if your faith was challenged or destroyed by these circumstances?

5. How do we respond when a friend, neighbor, or loved one faces such tragedy? How *should* we respond?

Encountering Scripture

In a nutshell Job is portrayed as "blameless and upright, one who feared God and turned away from evil" (Job 1:1).

One might suspect that such a heroic figure would garner only good fortune. Job's lot, however, was far from easy. Misfortune was heaped upon him as time after time adversity struck. Unjustly dealt with, Job cursed his life (Job 3:3 and following), but ultimately regained faith in God. Read Job 42:1-6.

The book of Job is rich and complex. It is well worth your time to read it in its entirety if you are not familiar with it. It is impossible to distill its wisdom to a few words (and I apologize for trying to do so now).

God's answer to Job was not easy. God's actions may be beyond our understanding. That does not mean that they are beyond the understanding of God. God is good; God is one.

Because God's wisdom is beyond us, we see meaningless suffering and reject it. But that is an incomplete response. In a great act of faith, we, like Job, must acknowledge our ignorance and yield to the wisdom, goodness, and power of the Lord.

BIBLE STUDY

Read again Job 3:20-23. Job poses a bitter question— ancient yet still urgent today. Why does God tolerate undeserved suffering?

Beneath this question looms an even more fundamental question: What is the meaning of faith?

BIBLE STUDY
Ask a group member to read this passage aloud.

WRITTEN REFLECTION

<u>Are there times when you can believe that God has an answer, even if you don't understand it? Are there times when you can't? What does it do to you when you can't believe that there is any meaning for the pain? How do you react then, if it is your pain? A loved one's?</u>

The question of undeserved suffering is critical in the New Testament. Read Matthew 27:22-50, which is Matthew's record of Jesus' last hours.

As you read, or hear this passage read aloud, put yourself in Jesus' place. Individually reflect on the questions below, recording your responses in the spaces provided.

How does it feel to be handed over to the mob?

How does it feel to be flogged?

How does it feel to be brutalized by the soldiers?

How does it feel to march to your death?

How does it feel to be nailed to the cross?

How does it feel to be mocked and taunted as you die?

How does it feel to have your final prayer misunderstood?

How does it feel to suffer undeservedly? To die undeservedly?

WORSHIP

BEFORE NEXT TIME

If your group has access to a piano or other musical accompaniment—or if your group is comfortable singing without accompaniment— begin your next session by singing some strengthening hymns.

1. What parallels do you see between our suffering in the face of an illness or disability, and Jesus' suffering on the cross? In what ways did he suffer the same as we do?

2. Did he endure more? How was Jesus' experience unique?

3. Might someone living with a debilitating disease or a prolonged illness know a different kind of pain than Jesus did?

Jesus suffered because he loved us. God suffers because God loves us. I confess, that, being weak of faith, I can imagine hurting so much that even the answer, "God loves us; God suffers with us," seems inadequate. I pray that I am spared those trials; I pray that my faith will be strengthened if they do come. But if they come, and if I fail, I pray that God, who is wise, and good, and great far beyond my comprehension, will have the answers that I lack. I pray that God will rescue me.

As you end this session, record the prayer concerns shared by members of your LIFESEARCH group:

In unison, pray this prayer:

Lord, we pray not for tranquility, nor that our tribulations may cease; we pray for thy Spirit and thy love, that thou grant us strength and grace to overcome adversity; through Jesus Christ. Amen.

Using a hymnal, scan the texts of hymns written to provide strength in tribulation. Discover these hymns by looking at the table of contents and index of your church's hymnal. As you look at these hymns, consider how these hymns might have encouraged suffering Christians.

CHAPTER THREE
DEATH—AND LIFE

CHECKING IN

Take time now to have persons share about their encounters and reflections upon health and wholeness since the last time you met as a LIFESEARCH group.

DISCUSSION POINT

How can we ease the pain of death? How can we keep it from stealing the life from us even before we die?

DISCUSSION POINT

What would you hope to find on your grave marker? Which of your virtues would be inscribed on your grave marker?

*By the sweat of your face
    you shall eat bread
until you return to the ground,
    for out of it you were taken;
you are dust,
    and to dust you shall return.*
                    (Genesis 3:19)

Death waits for each of us.

The fear of our own death can keep us from living fully. The pain of another's death can wound us beyond measure.

Every so often I like to visit old graveyards. There is a peace that rules over them, a peace that the living can share.

There once was a woman named Florence Dale Knoble, who lived from 1894 to 1952. Now her remains rest in a cemetery in Marion, Ohio. She died before I was born. I have never met anyone who knew her, but I did come upon her memorial a decade ago. On her gravestone the following words are engraved:

*Sweet rest, gentle lady!
Her home was ever a haven of peace, a refuge from weariness and care.
Her gentle voice can still be heard, her countless kindnesses recalled.
Loyal, serene, patient, brave.
Blessed are the pure in heart, for they shall see God.*

The world knows her now only for the virtues inscribed upon her grave marker. What a wonderful person she must have been! May we all be remembered for our virtues, and not our sins!

Those who die live on in the memories of the loved ones who survive them. <u>What remembrances do you have of someone whose gentle voice you still hear, whose countless kindnesses you recall?</u>

Modern Dying

You do not have to wander through many cemeteries before you realize that life was different a hundred years ago. Headstones tell of losing two, three, four children in infancy; mothers dying in childbirth and being buried with their babies; older brothers and sisters struck down in succession by whooping cough, diphtheria, or influenza.

Our forebears were intimately acquainted with death. With a shorter life expectancy, a much greater childhood mortality rate, and large extended families, most people, even in a small community, attended many funerals each year.

Contrast that with our experience today. Life expectancy in the United States is seventy-five years now—it was forty-five years at the turn of the century. The death of children is, fortunately, rare beyond the neonatal period, and the death rate for infants is astoundingly lower than it was then. Now, deaths occur primarily between the ages of sixty and eighty-five. Even in this age of automobile fatalities, AIDS deaths, and an increasing number of homicides, death rates of younger people are much lower than death rates for the older population. In contrast, a little more than a century ago, a twenty-five year old person, a thirty-five year old person, and a forty-five year old person all had the same chance of dying in the next year as did a sixty-five year old person—and that was quite a good chance indeed!

In the spaces below, reflect on your own experiences with death. You will not need to share these reflections unless you choose to do so. Review your own past experiences with death. Have you lost intimate family members or friends?

WRITTEN REFLECTION
Allow persons who wish to share their reflections to do so, but permit persons plenty of opportunity to "pass."

Other relatives or dear acquaintances?

Has death visited you frequently or rarely?

Did those deaths come suddenly, or was there time to prepare?

Have you ever had close contact with someone who knew they were dying?

Have you yourself ever come close to dying?

How did that change you?

In our time, to use an euphemism, many more of us "die of old age." That fact is a wonderful triumph of medicine. There are thousands of premature babies who would not have survived a day had they been born in 1883, but who will grow up to live long and productive lives because they were born in 1993 in the United States. But since we now are more likely to die at old age, we die when the ties of family and community may have already been loosened. In our mobile society, we may not have younger family members nearby to care for us when we are dying. Much of our dying is done in hospitals or institutions, rather than at home. One could argue that in the 1990's, many persons prefer to "institutionalize" the dying, just as our society used to institutionalize people suffering from Down's syndrome. As in other cases of segregation, both parties are harmed by the separation.

Most people who are dying want to have family and friends near in their final hours. It is clear what they lose when this does not happen. <u>But what about the living? What do we lose when we put death "out of sight?"</u>
Consider your "past history" with dying:

DISCUSSION POINT

Discuss the questions in the main text in groups of two or three.

1. Recall one of your experiences with death. <u>How did you feel? How did you react? How long did that event dominate your life?</u>

2. <u>How did that death change your thinking about your own life and death? How did it affect your relationship with others? With God?</u>

<u>Have you ever been unable to come to a loved one who was dying? How did you feel about not being able to be there?</u>

4. <u>Have you experienced the death of a loved one in a hospital or nursing home setting? Do you think they would have preferred to die at home? Why? How did the setting affect your relationship with your loved one at the end?</u>

DISCUSSION POINT

Have you known someone whose death seemed to come at just the right time?

What made it seem right?

Death can come at the "wrong time" (or at least it can seem that way from our limited human perspective), but it can come at the right time, too. A young woman who has for two years fought a losing battle against leukemia may have a different attitude towards death than she did before her illness.

An old man who has seen his wife and friends die before him does not look at death as he did when he was twenty. There is a reason why pneumonia used to be called "the old person's friend."

Biologists have discovered an enzyme called *superoxide dismutase* that is involved in repair of cellular damage. Organisms that lack the enzyme age rapidly. Some researchers have suggested that by activating the gene in humans, our life span could be markedly extended. They have nicknamed the gene for the enzyme the "Methuselah" gene.

DISCUSSION POINT

Would you volunteer for an experiment to test that hypothesis? What would be the consequences of an individual living to 150 years of age? What would be the consequences for society if *everybody* chose to take the "Methuselah" medicine?

What would you do, what would you want, how would you conduct your life, if you knew you only had a minute to live? A day? A month? A year? Ten years?

Sometimes death is sudden and quick; sometimes it comes after a long struggle. When death is prolonged, the reaction of other people can influence the manner of dying.

For instance, as a physician, I have an uneasy relationship with death. Health professionals develop attitudes towards death that are hard to shake. Death is the enemy. The death of my patient means that I have failed. Death brings emotions and situations with which I do not want to deal.

DISCUSSION POINT

Have you ever seen conflict develop over a dying person's final wishes?

How did the survivors feel about this afterwards?

Are there any changes that you might suggest in the way hospitals treat the dying?

Every nurse or physician at some time has similar thoughts. Many, many times I have heard a nurse or physician say, "He's not going to die while *I'm* on duty."

What happens when the patient is ready for death, but the physician is not? Sometimes, needless suffering can result.

DISCUSSION POINT

What are some of the advantages and disadvantages you can imagine with "living wills"?

Can you think of other ways to mediate conflicts between the living and the dying?

A *living will* is a legal instrument by which patients specify ahead of time what kind of treatment they do not want, should they ever be terminally ill and incapable of expressing personal desires at that time. They contain instructions such as, "I direct that the physicians supervising my care upon a terminal diagnosis discontinue hydration by intravenous fluids, should the continuation of such hydration be judged to result in unduly prolonging a natural death."

DISCUSSION POINT

Ask if any member of the group wishes to share how someone's suicide affected them as a survivor. Be sensitive during this person's sharing, as the memory of a family member's or friend's suicide may be painful.

For further information and discussion about some of the issues surrounding assisted suicide, you might want to look at the unit on "Life and Death" in Challenge *(Cokesbury, 1992).*

BIBLE STUDY

DISCUSSION POINT

Divide into smaller groups of three to five persons. Discuss the questions in the main text. If you want, record responses on newsprint or other writing surface as smaller groups share their reflections with the larger group.

WRITTEN REFLECTION

Provide paper and pencils for this activity.

Assisted suicide refers to someone, perhaps a loved one or a physician, helping a terminally ill person commit suicide when that person is not physically capable of doing it himself or herself.

How is the issue of assisted suicide different from that of unassisted suicide? How do you think society should address the practice of assisted suicide? How do you think the church should address this issue?

Encountering Scripture

Read 2 Samuel 12:15-23.

Consider this event from the perspective of David's servants. Was David's response to his child's illness a "natural" one? How about his reaction to the infant's death?

What do you make of such a person? Do you admire his response? Are you put off by it?

What do you think it might have been about David that caused him to respond in this way?

Now read John 11:1-45.

Using a separate piece of paper, write your own short paraphrased version of this story from John's Gospel.

▶

DISCUSSION POINT

Ask persons to share their retellings of the story of Lazarus with the whole group. Discuss: What themes emerge in these retellings of the story of Lazarus?

What are the most important points in this story for you?

What surprises you about this story?

What parts of this story are difficult for you? (Did you leave any of the difficult parts out of your retelling of the story?)

▶

DISCUSSION POINT

This story is told only in the Gospel of John. There are only two other Gospel stories of Jesus raising people from the dead (Luke 8:41-42, 49-56, and 7:11-15). Suppose that these narratives had not been included in the canon (those writings deemed authoritative from the early centuries of the Christian church). <u>What would have been lost from the gospel message because of such an omission?</u>

When Jesus said to Martha, "Your brother will rise again" (23), Martha understood Jesus to be talking about some time in the future: "I know that he will rise again in the resurrection on the last day." Jesus corrected her: "I *am* the resurrection and the life." (Italics are mine.) God is here and now—as he was with Abraham, Jacob, and Moses, with Martha and Lazarus, as God is now with us. Death is not the ultimate reality. God is.

The Genesis story of Adam and Eve is the story of a people who remove themselves from God, and who experience death as the final, insurmountable barrier between themselves and God's love.

The rest of the Bible is the story of God bringing us back. In Christ, the final barrier is destroyed. Death is not the end. We are back again with God. God never went away!

As Paul wrote in Romans 8:38-39: *"Neither death, nor life, nor angels, nor rulers, nor things present, nor things to come, nor powers, nor height, nor depth, nor anything else in all creation, will be able to separate us from the love of God in Christ Jesus our Lord."*

Hallelujah!

WORSHIP

As you prepare to end this session, share with each other prayer concerns, recording them in the space below:

Sing or read aloud these words of hope:

Hymn of Promise

In the bulb there is a flower; in the seed, an
*   apple tree;*
in cocoons, a hidden promise: butterflies will
*   soon be free!*
In the cold and snow of winter there's a spring
*   that waits to be,*
unrevealed until its season, something God alone
*   can see.*

There's a song in every silence, seeking word
*   and melody;*
there's a dawn in every darkness, bringing hope
*   to you and me.*
From the past will come the future; what it
*   holds, a mystery,*
unrevealed until its season, something God alone
*   can see.*

In our end is our beginning; in our time,
*   infinity;*
in our doubt there is believing; in our life,
*   eternity.*
In our death, a resurrection; at the last, a
*   victory,*
unrevealed until its season, something God alone
*   can see.*

HEALTH AND WHOLENESS

CHAPTER FOUR

HEALING

CHECKING IN

As you begin this session, invite members to update the group on prayer concerns from last week.

In Times of Illness

O God, who dost forgive our iniquities and
*   heal our diseases, we cry unto thee.*
*   Our strength has been brought low, and we*
*   know not what the future holds.*
*   In our bodies, there is pain; in our*
*   souls, anxiety and unrest.*
If it may be, restore us to health.
*   We ask no miracle of deliverance,*
*   and if in the order of nature our*
*   suffering must continue,*
*   help us to accept it without*
*   rebellion.*
If it must lead us toward the valley of the
*   shadow,*
*   help us to fear no evil,*
*   but to go bravely into thy nearer*
*   presence.*
In thy good keeping, all is well.
*   Into thy hands we commend our bodies and*
*   our spirits.*
*Do with us as thou wilt. **Amen.***

Georgia Harkness, USA, 20th century; Copyright © 1943 Whitmore and Stone, renewed 1970 Georgia Harkness. From *The Glory of God*, Abingdon Press.)

If you or someone you know needs healing, please share that with the group so that others may pray with you. You may want to record these prayer concerns in the margin.

Dimensions of Healing

The American Heritage Dictionary of the English Language (1969) gives the following definition for the verb "to heal":

heal—1. To restore to health; cure. **2.** To set right; amend. **3.** To rid of sin, anxiety, or the like; restore.

Thus, *to heal* is to restore, set right, or amend that which has been damaged or broken. We think of the body as being the object of healing, but if we ignore the mind and spirit, healing will not be complete. Sometimes, when we cannot restore the

DISCUSSION POINT

To what extent do you believe that money spent on health care is wisely or foolishly spent?

How do you feel when you acknowledge that life, your life, will end?

How does your faith enable you to understand your finitude?

body, the *only* way to set things right is to work directly with mind and soul.

Drugs, surgery, and radiation; gene therapy, physical therapy, and psychotherapy—these are some of the tools of modern medicine. Our society spends billions upon billions of dollars every year for health care—for healing care. Yet misfortune comes from having a body. The laws of nature do not bow down to our wishes, no matter how much money we spend. We exalt ourselves so much that we believe that we can and we will beat death.

Some persons assert that money on health care is foolishly spent. Worldwide, few of us live past the biblical "three score and ten." All of us die. Our pills and potions may change the moment of death, but cannot extend life forever.

All of us are familiar with healing, for all of us have experienced it in our own lives. Think about how many times you have cut, scraped, bruised, or burned yourself during your life. What would you look like now if your body had not healed? Our bodies repair and restore themselves constantly!

Different parts of our bodies heal differently. Skin cells regenerate faster than bone. Nerves heal slowly, and if brain tissue is lost, it cannot be replaced.

And just as different kinds of physical trauma result in different kinds of healing, the same is true of emotional and spiritual injury. Most damage is repaired quickly, but some wounds may stay with us all our lives.

Our Own Stories of Healing

GROUP INTERACTION

Divide into smaller groups of two or three persons. Ask each individual within these smaller groups to follow the instructions in the main text. Urge persons to be brief. You might want to keep time for the entire group, allowing each individual within each smaller group no more than five minutes before shifting to another person within their group.

Think about three healing events in your life. Choose one example of physical healing, emotional healing, and spiritual healing. Describe each in a few sentences. Then answer the following questions:

1. What was the nature of the precipitating illness or injury? Was it an accident? Was it inflicted on you by nature? By another person? Did you feel that you did anything to contribute to the problem? Did you feel guilt or shame about the experience?

2. How did the healing take place? Were there any false starts? Who was in charge of the healing? Did you feel that you had any degree of responsibility for it? How much of your time and energy did the healing consume? What effects did that have on the rest of your life at the time?

3. How does that healing experience affect your life now? How have your activities changed? Your relationships with others? Your general outlook on life? Your relationship with God?

4. If you had to live through that time again, what would you do differently? What would have made the experience easier or better for you? What would have made it easier or better for those who were with you?

As you discuss your answers with the group, explore any parallels between physical, emotional, and spiritual healing. <u>What kind of experiences seem to have the greatest positive effect? Which ones are the most difficult to get over? What attitudes toward healing seem to be most productive?</u>

DISCUSSION POINT

Discuss these questions within the whole group.

GROUP INTERACTION

Divide the larger group into new smaller groups of two or three persons. Ask each smaller group to discuss one of the case studies. Ask them to focus on the question: What examples of physical, emotional, or spiritual healing do you find in these actual case studies?

Paths to Healing

1. A mother brings her four-month-old baby girl to you, saying that she is afraid that she has become blind, though she seemed to have normal vision until this month. Tests run by neurologists and ophthalmologists at three different hospitals confirm the mother's worst fears—her baby cannot see. The mother mourns the loss of her "seeing" baby, but gradually both mother and child begin to adapt to the new reality.

When the baby is eight months old, the mother reports that she thinks her baby is once more responding to light. You examine the infant and see that this is so. By twelve months of age, the baby's vision is wholly restored, and she never has any problems with it again. No one can explain why she lost her vision, or why it returned.

2. An eight-year-old girl is brought to you because of a stomachache. Her exam is normal, except that she is constipated. You give her medicine and send her home.

The next day she returns in much more pain, and she is having fever and vomiting. It is obvious now that she has appendicitis. By the time she gets to surgery, the appendix has ruptured.

You and the surgeon treat her with intravenous antibiotics. In spite of appropriate care, the child continues to spike a fever and her pain gets worse. After seven days, a CT scan demonstrates an intra-abdominal abscess. The surgeon has to operate again. This time surgical drains are left in the wound, to help keep the abscess from reforming. The child is miserable.

Again she receives antibiotics. Again she fails to improve. After six more days, another CT scan shows that a new abscess has formed. You have never seen anyone with appendicitis follow such an awful course as this child has. Both you and the surgeon dread telling the little girl and her mother that she must go back to surgery a third time.

When you go to talk to her, both she and her mother are calm. The girl tells you that an angel came to her in a dream that afternoon. The angel said that she would have to have surgery one more time, but after that she would be well. A shiver runs down your spine.

The girl returns to the operating room and the abscess is drained. Her recovery, finally, is now uncomplicated. Ten days later she is able to leave the hospital.

3. A forty-year-old man is diagnosed as having a malignancy. He is told that he might die within a year. He goes into a deep depression. He skips his treatments and does not take his medications.

After four months the man's wife is successful in convincing him to join a psychotherapy group for people with cancer. He faithfully attends all of those sessions, though he still sometimes "forgets" his medical appointments. Gradually he comes out of his depression.

When he does, he shows a new attitude towards himself and his illness. He learns more than his doctors know about the benefits of good nutrition, exercise, and stress management in the treatment of cancer. He does not skip treatments or medicine. He finds time to do some things that he had always wanted to do, even though he is in pain.

4. A ten-month-old baby contracts herpes encephalitis. Before that time he was completely normal; after the illness he is devastated. He becomes blind, he loses the ability to babble, and he never regains any meaningful control of his arms and legs. He will be profoundly retarded. As he also lost the ability to swallow, he must be fed through a gastrostomy tube. You cannot imagine a worse fate.

His mother never falters. You have never seen anyone do a better job of caring for someone with such disabilities. She does not merely feed him and clean him. She takes him for walks. She takes him to church. She talks to him as if he understands her.

When he is three years old, she brings him to see you. She is beaming with pride. "Look," she says, "he smiles when I make a funny face!" You look at the boy and see nothing. It is a full year before you can recognize the smile that his mother proudly showed you.

5. A forty-five-year-old woman realizes that she is becoming more forgetful. For months she attributes it to "just being absent-minded." One day she becomes lost in her own neighborhood. The episode prompts her to see her physician. She is diagnosed as having early-onset Alzheimer's disease.

She is depressed and angry at the same time. Her condition deteriorates rapidly. Bit by bit, she observes her cognitive functions diminishing. She forgets people. She forgets whole periods of her life. She cannot even go unescorted to the ladies' room at a restaurant, for fear she will not be able to find her way back to the table.

After a year of rapid deterioration, she levels off on one of the "plateaus" typical of Alzheimer's disease. She knows that it is just a matter of time until she worsens again. She knows that eventually she will not be able to do anything for herself, and she will not even recognize the faces of the loved ones who will care for her. But for now the progression is slowed. And unlike many patients with Alzheimer's, she has retained good control of her speech. She feels the need to use all of her abilities *now*, for she does not know which ones will be gone tomorrow.

She writes a remarkable book about her experience with Alzheimer's disease, which will no doubt help thousands of fellow sufferers and their families deal with the illness. She knows that writing the book does not change her prognosis. (This book is *Living in the Labyrinth: A Journey Through the Maze of Alzheimer's Disease,* by Diana F. McGowin; Elder Books, 1993).

Each of these case studies is factual. Most of them occurred during my medical practice. One is the amazing story of an author suffering from Alzheimer's disease.

Perhaps these stories brought other examples of illness and healing to your mind. You might wish to take the time to pray at this moment for persons who now suffer.

God of compassion, source of life and health:
strengthen and relieve your servant(s) [NAMES],
and give your power of healing to those who minister to their needs,
that those for whom our prayers are offered
may find help in weakness
and have confidence in your loving care;
through him who healed the sick
and is the physician of our souls,
even Jesus Christ our Lord. Amen.

(From *The Book of Common Prayer*, alt. by Laurence Hull Stookey, alt. 1989 The United Methodist Publishing House.)

WORSHIP

When small groups have finished discussing the case studies, take a moment to pray for those who suffer, using the prayer printed in the main text.

BIBLE STUDY

GROUP INTERACTION

Divide into groups of three or four persons, with each group studying one of the miracles listed in the main text. Each smaller group should start by having one of their members read the passage aloud, or even better, by acting the story out. They should try to get a feel for the expectations, the hopes, and the fears of the people involved.

Then instruct them to read or act out the story again, this time focusing on the issues from Jesus' perspective.

Ask them to prepare answers to the questions in the main text.

Encountering Scripture

Luke 5:12-16, Jesus heals a man with leprosy.

Luke 5:17-26, Jesus heals a paralyzed man.

Luke 7:1-10, Jesus heals the centurion's servant.

Luke 17:11-19, Jesus heals ten men with leprosy.

John 5:2-17, Jesus heals a sick man at the pool of Beth-zatha.

Luke 22:47-51, Jesus heals the high priest's servant.

Jesus was a miracle worker. He calmed the storm; he walked on water. He turned water into wine. He fed five thousand people with five loaves and two fish.

None of us will ever turn water into wine; none of us will probably bring anyone who is truly dead back to life. But many of Jesus' miracles involved healing. And that is something that is close to us, for we all try to engage in healing—of ourselves, our friends and families, our churches, our communities, and our world. Let us read these Gospel stories to see what Jesus can teach us about working miracles.

1. How was this person suffering? What would it be like to experience that condition? Have you ever experienced something similar?

2. Why did the petitioner come to Jesus? What did he expect from Jesus? Did he get what he expected?

3. What did Jesus see in that person? Did he recognize something that had been overlooked? Did Jesus overlook anything in this person?

4. Did the person deserve to be healed? Did he deserve *not* to be healed? Did that influence Jesus' response to him?

5. Was Jesus responsible for this healing? Was the person healed in any way responsible for the healing? If so, how?

6. What did the healed person take away from this experience? Did this experience change Jesus,too? How did it affect the onlookers?

DISCUSSION POINT

Ask smaller groups to share their findings with the whole group.

DISCUSSION POINT

What does your own denomination and congregation believe about spiritual healing?

Does the hymn book that your congregation uses contain any healing services?

Have you participated in a service of healing?

If not, how comfortable do you think you would be to participate in such a service?

What might inhibit some persons from participating in a service of healing?

WORSHIP

So, how do we heal ourselves? How do we help to heal our neighbor?

• First, we must give up the self-righteousness that we put on to separate ourselves from others. Jesus was available to saint and sinner, rich and poor. Anybody could talk with him (and still can).

• Second, we must open our hearts to the "still, small voice" that makes the impossible possible. Our conception of what can or cannot happen is from the experience of humans, "but for God all things are possible" (Matthew 19:26).

• And finally, we must give up the kind of life that always fits us like a comfortable chair. We must get to work—we must go about the work of God. Jesus is no longer physically present to continue a healing ministry. We are the tools that he must use now. We are the body of Christ.

Ministries of spiritual healing have been a part of the Christian faith since the days of Jesus. Recently, however, many Christian bodies have renewed an interest in them. After years of looking askance at spiritual healing, several denominations have now incorporated services of healing into their worship resources. For example, The United Methodist Church has done so, prefacing its services of healing with these comments:

All healing is of God. The Church's healing ministry in no way detracts from the gifts God gives through medicine and psychotherapy. It is no substitute for either medicine or the proper care of one's health. Rather it adds to our total resources for wholeness.

Healing is not magic, but underlying it is the great mystery of God's love.

God does not promise that we shall be spared suffering but does promise to be with us in our suffering. Trusting that promise, we are enabled to recognize God's sustaining presence in pain, sickness, injury and estrangement.

(From *The United Methodist Book of Worship*, Abingdon, 1992; pages 613-14.)

As you end this session, use prayers or other portions of services of healing that you have available to you.

For background information regarding ministries of spiritual healing, you might want to read *Blessed to Be a Blessing* by James K. Wagner (The Upper Room, 1980).

CHAPTER FIVE

PERSONAL HEALTH

CHECKING IN

Check in with one another by asking group members to share significant occurrences in their lives since last time. Also ask them to comment briefly on their perceived health and wholeness (as they understand them at this point in the study).

WORSHIP

You may want to have on hand several copies of the same translation of the Bible (such as the New Revised Standard Version) if you plan to have the group read Psalm 14 in unison.

"All attachment to the senses is death."
—Mohandas Gandhi.

"Human infirmity in moderating and checking the emotions I name bondage; for, when a man is a prey to his emotions, he is not his own master, but lies at the mercy of fortune: so much so, that he is often compelled, while seeing that which is better for him, to follow that which is worse."
—Benedict de Spinoza, from *The Ethics of Human Bondage, on the Strength of Emotions (Part IV)*

"So you also must consider yourselves dead to sin and alive to God in Christ Jesus. Therefore, do not let sin exercise dominion in your mortal bodies, to make you obey their passions. No longer present your members to sin as instruments of wickedness, but present yourselves to God as those who have been brought from death to life, and present your members to God as instruments of righteousness."
—The apostle Paul, Romans 6:11-13.

We pray today for the strength to seek after God. For our opening prayer, turn to Psalm 14 and read the entire Psalm aloud.
You might also wish to pray "The Serenity Prayer":
God, grant me
> *the serenity to accept the things I cannot change,*
> *the courage to change the things I can,*
> *and the wisdom to distinguish the one from the other. Amen.*
(Anonymous, *The United Methodist Hymnal*, No. 459.)

The Strength of Emotions

We all have desires, emotions, passions. Sometimes these are quite base. What keeps us from acting on them? What keeps us from eating and drinking to excess? From indulging in the subtle pleasures of cocaine? From having our way with our neighbor? Yes, we all occasionally indulge in the forbidden. But why not go for *everything*? Suppose that no one would ever find out? That no one would ever tell you that you are wrong? That no one would ever show you a better way? Why not spend our lives trying to satisfy our appetite for meaningless diversions at the expense of others, until the day we die?

"If there is no God, then all things are permissible," wrote Dostoevsky in *The Brothers Karamazov*. What a bleak prospect!

Fortunately, my friends, we do have God.

Paul, Spinoza, Gandhi (the three persons quoted at the beginning of this chapter)—each of these "spiritually-intoxicated" souls lived a full, vibrant life, but a life clothed in the simplest of material trappings. Picture Paul sewing his tents, Spinoza grinding lenses, Gandhi at his spinning wheel. They did not hide from the world; rather, they immersed themselves in it, worked with it, battled it, and transformed it with their love. Paul spread the Word to the ends of the earth. Spinoza fought the political and religious powers of his day on behalf of freedom of thought and belief. Gandhi's nonviolent resistance of evil brought his country to freedom.

How could they have lived those lives without knowing joy and sorrow? Love and anger? Confidence and fear? They were human, not superhuman, and they must have felt the same hunger for satisfaction, success, and recognition as we do.

But look at their words again. Theirs is not a message to withdraw from the senses or to flee from emotion and passion—emotion and passion are the human experience. Instead, they warn us that giving ourselves over to passion leads to injury, illness, and death—both spiritually and physically.

This should not be news to us. How many Americans die each year as a result of their attachment to tobacco or alcohol? How many are shot to death in the heat of an argument? How many are crippled or die because of promiscuity? How often are families, friendships, and churches torn apart because of emotions and passions that are not held in check?

We cannot deny ourselves the joy that comes from having a body; neither can we hand ourselves over to the constant pursuit of pleasure. Both ways lead to death. Neither self-mortification nor self-indulgence can bring health or wholeness.

But perhaps, in the words of Paul, there is "a more excellent way" (1 Corinthians 12:31b).

Without giving any details, consider whether your answer to the following questions are *yes* or *no*. Consider sharing your answers with the group:

1. Have you ever done something for which you might have been arrested? Had a police officer observe you?

DISCUSSION POINT

Ask for any sharing, but do not press persons to say anything if they do not wish to.

DISCUSSION POINT

Ask members to discuss their responses to the extent they are comfortable doing so. Again, do not press persons to respond if they do not wish to.

WRITTEN REFLECTION

2. Has there been any period in your life when you indulged yourself to excess in many ways at once?

3. Have you recently done anything that you would be ashamed to confess to your pastor?

4. Have you ever in disgust sworn off a bad habit, only to find yourself being irresistibly drawn back to it later on?

5. Do you have any current vices that you have tried and failed to overcome?

6. Has your health ever suffered because you couldn't stop doing something you knew was bad for you?

I hope that many of you were able to give some *no* answers—but I confess that my answers to these questions were all *yes*.

For the final part of the exercise, consider this question: Why is it so difficult to behave? Write down three brief sentences in response. Invite members to share their thoughts with the group.

Creatures of Habit

How much of life is spent unconsciously repeating past routines! My morning paper and coffee, a quick breakfast, tooth brushing followed by a shower, the route I drive to work—the first two hours of my day are governed almost entirely by habit. Habit controls many of our food choices, our pattern of exercise, and how much sleep we get. For some persons, habit governs whether or not they smoke a cigarette after dinner or fix themselves a hot toddy before bed.

Habit also rules our interpersonal relationships. We gradually develop comfortable, predictable ways of dealing with family and friends. The patterns persist even when the people change dramatically. If you doubt this, attend your next high school reunion!

Habits certainly influence our health. The smoking habit kills more than one thousand Americans every day. Motorists who have the habit of using their seat belts and shoulder harnesses tend to live longer than those who do not. And in this decade, people with the habit of having sex with many partners may live very short lives indeed!

The habits associated with health, like those associated with unhealthiness, are not kept secret from us. The hard part is not knowing the right way to act, nor even acting the right way when we reflect upon it. The hard part is getting rid of our bad habits and assuming better habits, so that we routinely choose the healthy action even when we do not think about it.

WRITTEN REFLECTION

Allow time for group members to write their reflections individually, on newsprint or paper.

DISCUSSION POINT

Ask members to compare their responses with those of others in the group.

1. Make four lists:

a. Habits healthy for the body.
b. Habits unhealthy for the body.
c. Habits healthy for the soul.
d. Habits unhealthy for the soul.

Enter into each list five items that you think would apply for most people. Rank the items according to relative importance.

2. Make four more lists:

a. Healthy habits I have.
b. Unhealthy habits I don't have.
c. Healthy habits I want to develop.
d. Unhealthy habits I want to stop.

Put five entries from the first set of lists into the second set of lists, and order the entries according to their importance to your present and future health.

In the drug world, the word *habit* has at times been used to refer to a user's addiction. A heroin user might talk about stealing to support his or her habit. Certainly there is a world of difference between having the habit, say, of poor dental care, and the "habit" of shooting heroin. Addiction is often complicated by such issues as coexisting psychiatric disorders, loss of support mechanisms such as family and church, and pharmacologic tolerance of or dependence on the addicting drug. Indeed, most of medicine's efforts to fight addiction have failed miserably.

But if some people can throw off the chains of addiction to a deadly drug, can we take heart that many other "habits" can be reformed, also? There *is* a program that has been successful in helping people overcome one of the most intractable addictions that exists. That "habit" is alcoholism, and the program is Alcoholics Anonymous.

In 1935, a physician and a businessman began talking to each other about their inability to give up alcohol. Both had received the best medical treatment available, but they continued to drink. From their discussions was born a new way of fighting addiction. In the half-century since its birth, Alcoholics Anonymous (AA) has helped to keep millions of alcoholics sober. Its principles have been adopted into other programs to treat millions more suffering from other addictions, such as addictions to food, drugs, or gambling.

AA has a high initial dropout rate—50 percent of new members leave within the first 3 months. But for those who continue in "the fellowship," the success rate is amazing. Of those who can be found at any given meeting, about 35 percent have been sober less than 1 year, 36 percent have been sober between 1 and 5 years, and 29 percent have been sober more than 5 years. The average length of sobriety of the members is about 4 years.

Consider the lives saved! The goals accomplished! The love given! All by these men, women, and children who, because of Alcoholics Anonymous, are able to stay sober. And it all happened because of two drunkards! Two drunkards—and a Higher Power Christians know as God. Members of AA benefit from having a sponsor (mentor); some are aided by living in group homes. But the driving principles of the organization are put forward in THE TWELVE STEPS OF ALCOHOLICS ANONYMOUS:

1. We admitted we were powerless over alcohol—that our lives had become unmanageable.

2. Came to believe that a Power greater than ourselves could restore us to sanity.

3. Made a decision to turn our will and our lives over to the care of God as we understood Him.

4. Made a searching and fearless moral inventory of ourselves.

5. Admitted to God, to ourselves, and to another human being the exact nature of our wrongs.

6. Were entirely ready to have God remove all these defects of character.

7. Humbly asked Him to remove our shortcomings.

8. Made a list of all persons we had harmed, and became willing to make amends to them all.

9. Made direct amends to such people wherever possible, except when to do so would injure them or others.

10. Continued to take personal inventory and when we were wrong promptly admitted it.

11. Sought through prayer and meditation to improve our conscious contact with God, as we understood Him, praying only for knowledge of His will for us and the power to carry that out.

12. Having had a spiritual awakening as the result of these steps, we tried to carry this message to alcoholics, and to practice these principles in all our affairs.

(Statistics and this version of The Twelve Steps are reprinted from "Long-Term Recovery From Alcoholism," by J.Chappel, in *Recent Advances in Addictive Disorders*, edited by N. Miller; The Psychiatric Clinics of North America, 16:177-187, 1993.)

DISCUSSION POINT

Do you see ways in which these steps may be helpful in reforming unhealthy habits or developing healthier ones?

Pick one of the items from your lists of habits that you need to change (pages 38-39). How can you apply the principles of "The Twelve Steps" to achieving your goal?

BIBLE STUDY

GROUP INTERACTION

Roleplay the drama found in Mark 10:17-27. Ask members to take the parts of Jesus; the rich man; two disciples; and the narrator (who speaks all the words not in quotations.

DISCUSSION POINT

Discuss your thoughts in response to these underlined questions.

What an extraordinary confession! Whether or not alcohol addiction is our personal battle, we as Christians have increasingly become more comfortable in using these twelve steps. In particular, steps 2 through 11 reflect traditional Christian thinking:

Step 2: Christians believe that divine power is indeed greater than human power.

Step 3: Christians believe that conversion requires a turning toward God.

Steps 4-6: Christians believe in examination, confession, forgiveness, and renewal.

Steps 8-9: Like Zacchaeus (Luke 19:1-10), Christians believe in restitution.

Step 10: Christians have appreciated the need for *continual* confession, forgiveness, and restitution.

Step 11: Christians know the power of prayer and the value of a growing personal relationship with God.

Encountering the Word

Read Mark 10:17-27.

Consider the following questions in relation to Mark 10:17-27:

1. What good habits does this man have?

2. What good habits does he presently lack?

3. This story is also told in Matthew 19:16-30 and Luke 18:18-30. But Mark is the only evangelist to report that "Jesus, looking at him, loved him" (21a). Why do you think Mark felt it important to let us know this?

4. Suppose it was you who ran up and knelt before Jesus, and suppose that he spoke the words in verse 21 to you: "You lack one thing; go, sell what you own, and give the money to the poor, and you will have treasure in heaven; then come, follow me." How would you react? How *do* you react?

5. Consider Jesus' comments in verse 23-27. Is he saying that we cannot be saved? If we *can* be saved, on what or whom does our salvation depend?

Mark recorded that the man was shocked at Jesus' words "and went away grieving, for he had many possessions" (22).

That is the last we hear of him. I used to think that he did not come back to Jesus. But perhaps there is more to the tale than is told in Mark. Without God, all things are permissible. With God, all things are possible! What a difference! May God continue to look at us and love us, and may God bring us all to everlasting life.

DISCUSSION POINT

Do you think that God brought the man back?
Can you believe that God will bring us back, too?

Close your session by sharing joys and concerns about which you may wish to pray during the week ahead. Record those in the space below:

WORSHIP

Pray this prayer:

The Lord bless us and keep us. The Lord make his face to shine upon us and be gracious to us. The Lord lift up his countenance upon us and give us peace. Amen. (based on Numbers 6:24-26)

CHAPTER SIX

HEALTH AND SOCIETY

CHECKING IN

Before joining together in prayer to begin this session, ask your LIFESEARCH group members for updates on prayer concerns from last time.

DISCUSSION POINT

The apostle John teaches us that "God is love" (1 John 4:16). With that in mind, let us recall and reflect upon the apostle Paul's description of love:

Love is patient; love is kind; love is not envious or boastful or arrogant or rude. It does not insist on its own way; it is not irritable or resentful; it does not rejoice in wrongdoing, but rejoices in the truth. It bears all things, believes all things, hopes all things, endures all things. Love never ends (1 Corinthians 13:4-8).

In this chapter we will talk about increasing health and wholeness for others. The challenge is tremendous. Disease, decadence, and destruction are present wherever we look. Individuals are broken. Our society is fragmented. Its malaise is born from and reflected in the ills of its members. The community of nations is united in name only, and international efforts to relieve suffering seem often to result in more suffering.

Is this what God intends? How do we keep from shaking our heads and turning away? Is it *our* duty to try to bring health and wholeness to others? How do we develop the strength to accomplish that task?

GROUP INTERACTION

You may want to go over the three-point instructions printed in the main text with your group members. Note particularly that persons are to put the health issue of a friend or family member into first person language. This accomplishes two things: (1) It protects the identity of the friend or family member, and (2) It personalizes what might otherwise be left as the problem of someone else.

As your group engages in this process, if newsprint or chalkboard are available, chart the discussion, recording the public health issue and the preferred response.

DISCUSSION POINT

Today's Public Health Problems

1. Make a list of what you personally consider to be the five most important public health problems today. Compare your list with those of other members.

2. Present a public health problem that has become a personal health issue for a friend or a family member. Such problems might include: communicable diseases such as AIDS, teenage pregnancy, lack of health insurance, lack of health access, contamination of the environment, or the epidemic of violence in society. Do not mention names; instead, use the first-person point of view. For example, instead of saying, "One of my cousins has AIDS, and this is his story," say "I have AIDS, and this is my story."

3. Now (again using first-person point of view) tell how you would prefer other individuals and society as a whole to respond to your situation. Let others comment on your request. Is it reasonable? Practicable? What changes would have to take place before others could respond in the way you desire?

What public health problems were on your lists? There are so many that could be included! The basic necessities of food and shelter are lacking for many people throughout the world. The by-products of our advanced civilization are poisoning our food, water, and even the air we breathe. When wars are waged, civilian populations suffer more than the warring armies.

In our own country, drug addiction not only ruins the life of the addict, but it can lay a claim on many around her or him— friends, family, or children, as well as the victims of the crimes she committed because of and for drugs. Early and promiscuous sexual activity results in an ever-increasing incidence of low-birth-weight and premature babies. Medical treatment for those babies is extraordinarily costly, and even though more and more survive, they have a much greater chance of long-term disability than do babies born healthy and at term. The AIDS epidemic shows no hint of abating. Alcohol and tobacco abuse generates disease that consumes billions of health dollars yearly.

GROUP INTERACTION

Divide the larger group into smaller groups of two or three persons. Ask each group to discuss one of the case studies. Questions to address appear after the fifth case study.

Case Studies

Note: The first four patients mentioned in these case studies appeared within a one-month period at an inner-city hospital in a medium-sized southern city. The fifth patient is a composite of several patients. These fact-based case studies may help "flesh out" problems of increasing health and wholeness for others in society at large.

(1) A three-year-old boy is brought into a children's clinic by his aunt, who does not have legal custody. The boy is happy and playful. He does not appear ill. His aunt asks you to start the boy on the medicine he needs. She says that he is HIV-positive (he has the AIDS virus) and that his mother (according to the aunt, HIV-negative) refuses to bring him in for medical care. Review of the boy's medical records confirms that he was diagnosed two months ago and has missed three appointments since.

(2) You are called to the emergency room of a hospital to evaluate an eighteen-month-old girl who presents with a burn injury to her left leg. The mother says that she found the child's five-year-old brother holding the little girl under running hot water. Examination of the toddler shows second- and third-degree burns to all of the left leg below the knee. The border between burned and unburned skin is a straight line around the leg. There are no splash marks. You believe that the mother's story is inconsistent with the appearance of the child's burn.

(3) You are called to the hospital nursery to examine a newborn baby girl. The baby's mother is HIV-positive. You order that the appropriate blood tests be done on the infant to see if she also carries the AIDS virus. An hour later the nursery contacts you again. The laboratory personnel have not been successful in drawing the infant's blood. If you want the tests done, you will need to draw blood from the baby yourself. You recall that you suffered an accidental needle stick last month when drawing blood from another child.

(4) A fourteen-year-old boy is transferred to the pediatric ward from the intensive care unit after he is over the acute effects of an overdose of cocaine. When you try to place him in a drug rehabilitation program, you find that none will take him because the family has no insurance. The Department of Human Services refuses to get involved, as no abuse is alleged. The boy denies that he has any problems. He wants to go home. The boy's mother tells you that she cannot control him. The last time she left him alone at home, she returned to find that he had sold their television, presumably for drug

money. You are convinced that the boy will be mainlining cocaine in a matter of hours if he is discharged home. Your hospital cannot provide rehabilitation services. You are asked repeatedly why you have not discharged the patient.

(5) You are in the emergency room of a hospital, treating another patient when a gunshot victim is wheeled in. He has obviously lost a large amount of blood from an abdominal wound. The policeman who was the first on the scene reports that the man was shot when a drug deal went bad. You note "needle tracks" on the patient's arms and legs. You see a scar on his chest and realize that you treated this man less than a month ago for a stab wound. You know that you have the skill to save him. But as you begin to work, the thought comes to you that no one will question your care if this patient dies.

DISCUSSION POINT

Consider the following questions with respect to each case study:

1. Who is the patient? Is there more than one person in need of healing in this situation? If there is more than one patient, what conflicts will arise from treating all of them?

2. Which individuals are responsible for their situation? Which ones are not? Should the patient's degree of responsibility for his or her suffering change the way we respond to it? In what way?

3. Does a Christian approach to these problems always imply an individual response, or are there times when it is right to let an organization, government agency, or other person or group handle the problem? How should we respond when those parties "drop the ball"?

4. Caregivers often experience "burnout" when working on cases such as these. How do we strike a balance between our problems and those of others? When should nurses, social workers, or physicians leave their patients at the hospital and go home to their own families? Can a Christian really set limits on how much she or he will do for others? What might such limits be?

Sin and Society

The problems identified so far in this session have something in common. The lifestyles or behaviors are well known to be injurious to individuals and society. Sages have counselled against them for centuries. Even those who practice these habits generally do not recommend them to others.

Take a moment to define the word *sin*. Write your definition in the space below.

In the Christian view, these activities are thought of as opposing God's purposes. Their fruit is known to be poison. These activities, simply put, represent sin.

This is not the same as saying that disease is a punishment from God. The just and unjust alike know illness. Saints and sinners all eventually suffer a real, physical death.

But the choices we make in life do influence the health and wholeness of ourselves and others. And often we choose wrong—we choose to sin, while we deny that we have any choice at all. The consequences of sin add up, producing misery upon misery that no one intended.

It is easy to feel "put upon" when we look at the ills of our society. It seems that we are being forced to clean up someone else's mess. <u>Taking responsibility for my own sins is one thing, but must I be responsible for the sins of others? Why can't people just behave? Why do I have to pay when they don't?</u>

Encountering the Scripture

Read Exodus 20:5-6 and John 9:1-4.

These readings present two strikingly different aspects of God. <u>Was Jesus declaring a new order? Was he pointing out something that was present all along, but overlooked?</u>

WRITTEN REFLECTION

Consider these two biblical passages with respect to the case studies presented earlier. Then write down your responses to the following questions:

1. To what extent is it right to hold people responsible for their actions? Are there times when *not* doing that contributes to the problem?

2. Can you think of examples of children seeming to be punished by God for the iniquity of their parents? Can you think of times when *you* have blamed children for the sins of their parents?

3. What was the most important issue for Jesus? How do we apply his words to dealing with the health problems you listed earlier?

4. *"We must work the works of him who sent me while it is day; night is coming when no one can work. As long as I am in the world, I am the light of the world"* (John 9:4-5). Does it bother you that the work is so great, or that "night is coming" whatever we do? How do we keep from giving up or giving in? How did Jesus keep to the goal? Does his promise in this passage give you hope?

"As long as I am in the world, I am the light of the world" (John 9:5). Jesus also said, *"I am with you always, to the end of the age"* (Matthew 28:20). As long as we are in the world, God has provided help to do God's work. There is no need to despair! We do not work for naught: we do not work alone. We do God's work, in God's kingdom, with the Holy Spirit at our side.

God bless you in your work towards health and wholeness!

WORSHIP

As you close this session, share prayer concerns and joys with one another. Record them in the space below.

Covenant to continue to pray for and with each other in the days to come. Consider ways in which you might continue to work on issues of health and wholeness in your individual lives and in your life together.

Pray this prayer together:

Come, my Light, and illumine my darkness.
Come, my Life, and revive me from death.
Come, my Physician, and heal my wounds.
Come, Flame of Divine Love, and burn up the thorns of my sins,
kindling my heart with the flame of thy love.
Come, my King, sit upon the throne of my heart and reign there.
For thou alone art my King and my Lord.
Amen.
—Dimitri of Rostov, Russia, 17th Century

(From *The Orthodox Way*, Kallistos Ware, 1979; Reproduced by permission of A. R. Mowbray & Co., Ltd.)

THE LIFESEARCH GROUP EXPERIENCE

Every LIFESEARCH group will be different. Because your group is made up of unique individuals, your group's experience will also be unique. No other LIFESEARCH group will duplicate the dynamics, feelings, and adventures your group will encounter.

And yet as we planned LIFESEARCH, we had a certain vision in mind about what we hoped might happen as people came together to use a LIFESEARCH book for discussion and support around a common concern. Each LIFESEARCH book focuses on some life concern of adults within a Christian context over a six-session course. LIFESEARCH books have been designed to be easy to lead, to encourage group nurture, and to be biblically based and needs-oriented.

Each chapter in this LIFESEARCH book has been designed for use during a one and one-half hour group session. In each LIFESEARCH book, you will find
• times for group members to "check in" with each other concerning what has gone on in their lives during the past week and what they wish to share from the past week concerning the material covered in the group sessions;
• times for group members to "check in" about how they are doing as a group;
• substantial information/reflection/discussion segments, often utilizing methods such as case studies and simulation;
• Bible study segments;
• segments in which a specific skill or

process is introduced, tried out, and/or suggested for use during the week to come;
• segments that help group participants practice supporting one another with the concerns being explored.

LIFESEARCH was not planned with the usual one hour Sunday school class in mind. If you intend to use LIFESEARCH with a Sunday school class, you will need to adapt it to the length of time you have available. Either plan to take more than one week to discuss each chapter or be less ambitious with what you aim to accomplish in a session's time.

LIFESEARCH was also not planned to be used in a therapy group, a sensitivity group, or an encounter group.

No one is expected to be an expert on the topic. No one is expected to offer psychological insights into what is going on. However, we do hope that LIFESEARCH group members will offer one another support and Christian love.

> A LIFESEARCH group is simply a group of persons who come together to struggle together from a Christian perspective with a common life concern.

We will count LIFESEARCH as successful if you find your way to thought-provoking discussions centered around information, insights, and helps providing aid for living everyday life as Christians.

You might find it helpful to see what we envisioned a sample LIFESEARCH group might experience. Keep in mind, however, that your experience might be quite different. Leave room for your creativity and uniqueness. Remain receptive to God's Spirit.

You sit in the living room of a friend from church for the second session of your LifeSearch group. Besides you and your host, four other persons are present, sitting on the sofa and overstuffed chairs. You, your host, your group leader, and one other are church members, although not all of you make it to church that regularly. The remaining two persons are neighbors of the leader. You chat while a light refreshment and beverage are served by the host.

Your leader offers a brief prayer, and then asks each of you to share what has been going on in your lives during the past week since you last met. One member shares about a spouse who had outpatient surgery. Several mention how hectic the week was with the usual work- and family-related demands. Prayer concerns and requests are noted.

This session begins with a written reflection. The leader draws your attention to a brief question in the beginning of the chapter you were assigned to read for today. Group members are asked to think about the question and write a short response.

While the leader records responses on a small chalkboard brought for that purpose, members take turns sharing something from their written reflections. A brief discussion follows when one group member mentions something she had never noticed before.

Group members respond as the leader asks for any reports concerning trying out the new life skill learned in the previous session. Chuckles, words of encouragement, and suggestions for developing the new skill further pepper the reports.

The leader notes one of the statements made in the assigned chapter from the LifeSearch book and asks to what extent the statement is true to the experience of the group members. Not much discussion happens on this point, since everyone agrees the statement is true. But one of the members presses on to the next statement in the LifeSearch book, and all sorts of conversation erupts! All six group members have their hot buttons pushed.

Your leader calls the group to move on to Bible study time. You read over the text, and then participate in a dramatic reading in which everyone has a part. During the discussion that follows the reading, you share some insights that strike you for the first time because you identify with the person whose role you read.

You and the other group members take turns simulating a simple technique suggested in the book for dealing with a specific concern. Everyone coaches everyone else; and what could have been an anxiety-producing experience had you remained so self-conscious, quickly becomes both fun and helpful. You and one of the other group members agree to phone each other during the week to find out how you're doing with practicing this technique in real life.

It's a few minutes later than the agreed upon time to end, but no one seems to mind. You read together a prayer printed at the end of this week's chapter.

On the way out to your car, you ponder how quickly the evening has passed. You feel good about what you've learned and about deepening some new friendships. You look forward to the next time your LifeSearch group meets.

This has been only one model of how a LifeSearch group session might turn out. Yours will be different. But as you give it a chance, you will learn some things and you will deepen some friendships. That's what you started LifeSearch for anyway, isn't it?

STARTING A LIFESEARCH GROUP

The key ingredient to starting a LIFESEARCH group is *interest*. People are more likely to get excited about those things in which they are interested. People are more likely to join a group to study and to work on those areas of their lives in which they are interested.

Interest often comes when there is some itch to be scratched in a person's life, some anxiety to be soothed, or some pain to be healed.

Are persons interested in the topic of a LIFESEARCH book? Or, perhaps more important to ask, do they have needs in their lives that can be addressed using a LIFESEARCH book?

If you already have an existing group that finds interesting one of the topics covered by the LIFESEARCH books, go for it! Just keep in mind that LIFESEARCH is intended more as a small-group resource than as a class study textbook.

If you want to start a new group around LIFESEARCH, you can begin in one of two ways:

- You can begin with a group of interested people and let them choose from among the topics LIFESEARCH offers; or

- You can begin with one of the LIFE-SEARCH topics and locate people who are

> **Interest often comes when there is some itch to be scratched in a person's life, some anxiety to be soothed, or some pain to be healed.**

interested in forming a group around that topic.

What is the right size for a LIFESEARCH group? Well, how many persons do you have who are interested?

Actually, LIFESEARCH is intended as a *small-group* resource. The best size is between four and eight persons. Under four persons will make it difficult to carry out some of the group interactions. Over eight and not everyone will have a good opportunity to participate. The larger the group means the less time each person has to share.

If you have more than eight persons interested in your LIFE-SEARCH group, why not start two groups?

Or if you have a group larger than eight that just does not want to split up, then be sure to divide into smaller groups of no more than eight for discussion times. LIFESEARCH needs the kind of interaction and discussion that only happen in small groups.

How do you find out who is interested in LIFESEARCH? One good way is for you to sit down with a sheet of paper and list the names of persons whom you think might be interested. Even better would be for you to get one or two other people to brainstorm names with you. Then start asking. Call them on the telephone. Or visit them in person. People respond more readily to personal invitations.

When you invite persons and they seem interested in LIFESEARCH, ask them if they will commit to attending all six sessions. Emergencies do arise, of course. However, the group's life is enhanced if all members participate in all sessions.

LIFESEARCH is as much a group experience as it is a time for personal learning.

As you plan to begin a LIFESEARCH group, you will need to answer these questions:

- **Who will lead the group?** Will you be the leader for all sessions? Do you plan to rotate leadership among the group members? Do you need to recruit an individual to serve as group leader?

- **Where will you meet?** You don't have to meet at a church. In fact, if you are wanting to involve a number of persons not related to your church, a neutral site might be more appropriate. Why not hold your meetings at a home? But if you do, make sure plans are made to hold distractions and interruptions to a minimum. Send the children elsewhere and put the answering machine on. Keep any refreshments simple.

- **How will you get the LIFESEARCH books to group members before the first session?** You want to encourage members to read the first chapter in advance of the first session. Do you need to have an initial gathering some days before the first discussion sessions in order to hand out books and take care of other housekeeping matters? Do you need to mail or otherwise transport the books to group members?

Most LIFESEARCH groups will last only long enough to work through the one LIFESEARCH book in which there is interest. Be open, however, to the possibility of either continuing your LIFESEARCH group as a support group around the life issue you studied, or as a group to study another topic in the LIFESEARCH series.

TIPS FOR LIVELY DISCUSSIONS

Recognize when the silence has gone on long enough. Some questions do fall flat. Some questions exhaust themselves. Some silence means that people really have nothing more to say. You'll come to recognize different types of silences with experience.

Don't lecture. You are responsible for leading a discussion, not for conveying information.

If Plan A doesn't work to stimulate lively discussion, move on to Plan B. Each chapter in this LIFESEARCH book contains more discussion starters and group interaction ideas than you can use in an hour and a half. If something doesn't work, move on and try something else.

Ask open-ended questions. Ask: How would you describe the color of the sky? Don't ask: Is the sky blue?

Allow silence. Sometimes, some people need to think about something before they say anything. The WRITTEN REFLECTIONS encourage this kind of thought.

Let the group lead you in leading discussion. Let the group set the agenda. If you lead the group in the direction you want to go, you might discover that no one is following you. You are leading to serve the group, not to serve yourself.

Ask follow-up questions. If someone makes a statement or offers a
response, ask: Why do you say
that? Better yet, ask a different
group member: What do you think
of so-and-so's statement?

Do your own homework. Read the
assigned chapter. Plan out possible
directions for the group session to
go based on the leader's helps in
the text. Plan options in case your
first plan doesn't work out. Know
the chapter's material.

Know your group. Think about the
peculiar interests and needs of the
specific individuals within your
group. Let your knowledge of the
group shape the direction in which
you lead the discussion.

Don't try to accomplish everything.
Each chapter in this LifeSearch
book offers more leader's helps in
the form of DISCUSSION POINTS,
GROUP INTERACTIONS, and
other items than you can use in one
session. So don't try to use them
all! People become frustrated with
group discussions that try to cover
too much ground.

Don't let any one person dominate
the discussion—including yourself.
(See "Dealing with Group Problems," page 58.")

Encourage, but don't force, persons
who hold back from participation.
(See "Dealing with Group Problems," page 58.)

TAKING YOUR GROUP'S TEMPERATURE

How do you tell if your LIFESEARCH group is healthy? If it were one human being, you could take its temperature with a thermometer and discover whether body temperature seemed to be within a normal range. Taking the temperature of a group is more complex and less precise. But you can try some things to get a sense of how healthily your group is progressing.

✔ **Find out whether the group is measuring up to what the members expected of it.** During the CHECKING IN portion of the first session, you are asked to record what members say as they share why they came to this LIFESEARCH group. At a later time you can bring out that sheet and ask how well the LIFESEARCH experience measures up to satisfying why people came in the first place.

✔ **Ask how members perceive the group dynamics.** Say: On a scale from one as the lowest to ten as the highest, where would you rate the overall participation by members of this group? On the same scale where would you rate this LIFESEARCH group as meeting your needs? On the same scale where would you rate the "togetherness" of this LIFESEARCH group?

You can make up other appropriate questions to help you get a sense of the temperature of the group.

✔ **Ask group members to fill out an evaluation sheet on the LIFESEARCH experience.** Keep the evaluation form simple.

One of the simplest forms leaves plenty of blank space for responding to three requests: (1) Name the three things you would want to do more of. (2) Name the three things you would want to do less of. (3) Name the three things you would keep about the same.

✔ **Debrief a LIFESEARCH session with one of the other participants.** Arrange ahead of time for a group member to stay a few minutes after a meeting or to meet with you the next day. Ask for direct feedback about what seemed to work or not work, who seems to be participating well, who seems to be dealing with something particularly troubling, and so forth.

✔ **Give group members permission to say when they sense something is not working.** As the group leader, you do not hold responsibility for the life of the group. The group's life belongs to *all* the members of the group. Encourage group members to take responsibility for what takes place within the group session.

✔ **Expect and accept that, at times, discussion starters will fall flat, group interaction will seem stilted, group members will be grumpy**. All groups have bad days. Moreover all groups go through their own life cycles. Although six sessions may not be enough time for your LIFESEARCH group to gel completely, you may find that after two or three sessions, one session will come when nothing seems to go right. That is normal. In fact, studies show that only those groups that first show a little conflict

56

ever begin to move into deeper levels of relationship.

✔ **Sit back and observe.** In the middle of a DISCUSSION POINT or GROUP INTER-ACTION, sit back and try to look at the group as a whole. Does it look healthy to you? Is one person dominating? Does someone else seem to be withdrawn? How would you describe what you observe going on within the group at that time?

✔ **Take the temperature of the group—really!** No, not with a thermometer. But try asking the group to take its own tempera-ture. Would it be normal? below normal? feverish? What adjective would you use to describe the group's temperature?

✔ **Keep a temperature record.** At least keep some notes from session to session on how you think the health of the group looks to you. Then after later sessions, you can look back on your notes from earlier sessions and see how your group has changed.

LifeSearch Group Temperature Record

Chapter 1
_____
_____
_____
_____

Chapter 4
_____
_____
_____
_____

Chapter 2
_____
_____
_____
_____

Chapter 5
_____
_____
_____
_____

Chapter 3
_____
_____
_____
_____

Chapter 6
_____
_____
_____
_____

DEALING WITH GROUP PROBLEMS

What do you do if your group just does not seem to be working out?

First, figure out what is going on. The ideas in "Taking Your Group's Temperature" (pages 56-57) will help you to do this. If you make the effort to observe and listen to your group, you should be able to anticipate and head off many potential problems.

Second, remember that the average LIFE-SEARCH group will only be together for six weeks—the average time needed to study one LIFESEARCH book. Most new groups will not have the chance to gel much in such a short period of time. Don't expect the kind of group development and nurture you might look for in a group that has lived and shared together for years.

Third, keep in mind that even though you are a leader, the main responsibility for how the group develops belongs to the group itself. You do the best you can to create a hospitable setting for your group's interactions. You do your homework to keep the discussion and interactions flowing. But ultimately, every member of the group individually and corporately bear responsibility for whatever happens within the life of the group.

However, if these specific problems do show up, try these suggestions:

✔ One Member Dominates the Group

• Help the group to identify this problem for itself by asking group members to state on a scale from one as the lowest to ten as the highest where they would rank overall participation within the group.

• Ask each member to respond briefly to a DISCUSSION POINT in a round robin fashion. It may be helpful to ask the member who dominates to respond toward the end of the round robin.

• Practice gate-keeping by saying, "We've heard from Joe; now what does someone else think?"

• If the problem becomes particularly troublesome, speak gently outside of a group session with the member who dominates.

✔ One Member Is Reluctant to Participate

• Ask each member to respond briefly to a DISCUSSION POINT in a round robin fashion.

• Practice gate-keeping for reluctant participants by saying, "Sam, what would you say about this?"

• Increase participation by dividing the larger group into smaller groups of two or three persons.

✔ The Group Chases Rabbits Instead of Staying With the Topic

• Judge whether the rabbit is really a legitimate or significant concern for the group to be discussing. By straying from your agenda, is the group setting an agenda more valid for their needs?

- Restate the original topic or question.

- Ask why the group seems to want to avoid a particular topic or question.

- If one individual keeps causing the group to stray inappropriately from the topic, speak with him or her outside of a session.

✔ Someone Drops Out of the Group

- A person might drop out of the group because his or her needs are not being met within the group. You will never know this unless you ask that person directly.

- Contact a person immediately following the first absence. Otherwise they are unlikely to return.

✔ The Group or Some of Its Members Remain on a Superficial Level of Discussion

- In a six-session study, you cannot necessarily expect enough trust to develop for a group to move deeper than a superficial level.

- Never press an individual member of a LIFESEARCH group to disclose anything more than they are comfortable doing so in the group.

- Encourage an atmosphere of confidentiality within the group. Whatever is said within the group, stays within the group.

✔ Someone Shares a Big, Dangerous, or Bizarre Problem

- LIFESEARCH groups are not therapy groups. You should not take on the responsibility of "fixing" someone else's problem.

- Encourage a member who shares a major problem to seek professional help.

- If necessary, remind the group about the need for confidentiality.

- If someone shares something that endangers either someone else or himself/herself, contact your pastor or a professional caregiver (psychologist, social worker, physician, attorney) for advice.

IF YOU'RE <u>NOT</u> LEADING THE GROUP

> **Be sure to read this article if you are *not* the person with specific responsibility for leading your LIFESEARCH group.**

If you want to get the most out of your LIFESEARCH group and this LIFESEARCH book, try the following suggestions.

✔ **Make a commitment to attend all the group sessions and participate fully.** An important part of the LIFESEARCH experience takes place within your group. If you miss a session, you miss out on the group life. Also, your group will miss what you would have added.

✔ **Read the assigned chapter in your LIFESEARCH book ahead of time.** If you are familiar with what the MAIN TEXT of the LIFESEARCH book says, you will be able to participate more fully in discussions and group interactions.

✔ **Try the activities suggested in BEFORE NEXT TIME.** Contributions you make to the group discussion based upon your experiences will enrich the whole group. Moreover, LIFESEARCH will only make a real difference in your life if you try out new skills and behaviors outside of the group sessions.

✔ **Keep confidences shared within the group.** Whatever anyone says within the group needs to stay within the group. Help make your group a safe place for persons to share their deeper thoughts, feelings, and needs.

✔ **Don't be a "problem" participant.** Certain behaviors will tend to cause difficulties within the life of any group. Read the article on "Dealing with Group Problems," on pages 58-59. Do any of these problem situations describe you? Take responsibility for your own group behavior, and change your behavior as necessary for the sake of the health of the whole group.

✔ **Take your turn as a group leader, if necessary.** Some LIFESEARCH groups will rotate group leadership among their members. If this is so for your LIFESEARCH group, accept your turn gladly. Read the other leadership articles in the back of this LIFESEARCH book. Relax, do your best, and have fun leading your group.

✔ **Realize that all group members exercise leadership within a group.** The health of your group's life belongs to all the group members, not just to the leader alone. What can you do to help your group become healthier and more helpful to its members? Be a "gatekeeper" for persons you notice are not talking much. Share a thought or a feeling if the discussion is slow to start. Back off from sharing your perspective if you sense you are dominating the discussion.

✔ **Take responsibility for yourself.** Share concerns, reflections, and opinions related to the topic at hand as appropriate. But keep in mind that the group does not exist to "fix" your problems. Neither can you "fix" anyone else's problems, though from time to time it may be appropriate to share insights on what someone else is facing based upon your own experience and wisdom. Instead of saying, "What you need to do is . . ." try saying, "When I have faced a similar situation, I have found it helpful to . . ."

✔ **Own your own statements.** Instead of saying, "Everyone knows such and so is true," try saying "I believe such and so is true, because . . . ." Or instead of saying "That will never work," try saying, "I find it hard to see how that will work. Can anyone help me see how it might work?" Instead of saying, "That's dumb!" try saying, "I have a hard time accepting that statement because . . . ."

OUR LifeSearch GROUP

Name   **Address**   **Phone Number**

_____

_____

_____

_____

_____

_____

_____

_____

_____

_____

_____

_____

FEEDBACK MAIL-IN SHEET

✂ CUT HERE

Please tell us what you liked and disliked about LIFESEARCH:

4. The two things I like best about this LIFESEARCH experience were

5. The two things I liked least about this LIFESEARCH experience were

6. The two things I would have done differently if I had designed this LIFESEARCH book are

7. Topics for which you should develop new LIFESEARCH books are

8. I want to be sure to say the following about LIFESEARCH.

9. I led _____ sessions of this LIFESEARCH book.

FOLD HERE

Thank you for taking the time to fill out and return this feedback questionnaire.

Please check the LIFESEARCH book you are evaluating.

☐ Spiritual Gifts   ☐ Health and Wholeness
☐ Juggling Demands   ☐ Stress
☐ Parenting   ☐ The Environment

Please tell us about your group:

1. Our group had an average attendance of _____ .

2. Our group was made up of
   _____ young adults (19 through 25 years of age).
   _____ adults mostly between 25 and 45 years of age.
   _____ adults mostly between 45 and 60 years of age.
   _____ adults 60 and over.
   _____ a mixture of ages.

3. Our group (answer as many as apply)
   _____ came together for the sole purpose of studying this LIFESEARCH book.
   _____ has decided to study another LIFESEARCH book.
   _____ is an ongoing Sunday school class.
   _____ met at a time other than Sunday morning.
   _____ had only one leader for this LIFESEARCH study.

Name_____

Address_____

_____

Telephone_____

Editor, LIFESEARCH series
Church School Publications
P. O. Box 801
Nashville, Tennessee 37202

STAPLE OR TAPE HERE